· CREATIVE CRAFTS ·

FUN WITH
FABRIC

· JULIET BAWDEN ·

HAMLYN

HANDY HINTS

This book gives you lots of wonderful ideas on how to make all sorts of things with different kinds of fabric. You can make them exactly as they are in the book, or you can use the ideas to make up your own special designs or projects.

Most of them are easy to make yourself, but you may need an adult to help when you are cutting out especially tricky or fiddly shapes. Or when you are sewing things together with a special type of stitch, such as a blanket stitch.

ACKNOWLEDGEMENTS

Projects made by Jan Bridge
and Anne Sharples
Photographs by David Johnson
Illustrations by Joanna Venus

HAMLYN CHILDREN'S BOOKS
Series Editor : Anne Civardi
Series Designer : Anne Sharples
Production Controller : Linda Spillane

Published in 1993 by
Hamlyn Children's Books
an imprint of Reed Children's Books,
Michelin House, 81 Fulham Road, London SW3 6RB
and Auckland, Melbourne, Sydney and Toronto

Paperback edition published in 1994.

ISBN 0 600 58353 8

British Library Cataloguing-in-Publication Data.
A catalogue record for this book is available from the British Library.

Books printed and bound in Italy

CONTENTS

MATERIALS, TIPS AND HINTS

This book shows you how to make all sorts of wonderfully original things using different types of fabric. It gives you ideas on how to decorate them with special fabric paints, felt tip pens, glitter and puff paints, as well as sequins, diamantés, buttons and beads.

For many of the projects you can use scraps of fabric you can find around the house, but for some you may need to buy bigger pieces of fabric. The special techniques include simple appliqué, tie-dyeing, easy weaving, and printing on fabric with vegetables and spaghetti.

Things to collect

Scraps of plain or patterned fabric
Scraps of brightly-coloured felt
Old buttons
Coloured ribbon and string
Sequins and beads
Stiff card
Embroidery thread in
    different colours
Small balls of brightly-
    coloured wool
Old baseball caps
    or berets
Old blue jeans

Useful tips

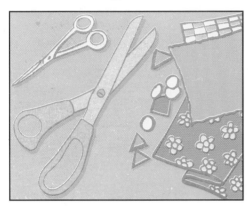

1. You will need a big pair of scissors for cutting big pieces of fabric and a small pair for small, fiddly things. Be very careful when you are using them.

2. It is very useful to have a pair of pinking shears, especially for cutting out felt shapes, other non-fraying fabrics, for the ends of ribbons and for decoration.

3. There are many special kinds of fabric paints and pens. You can find them in different shops. Try experimenting with puffy paints and glitter paints too.

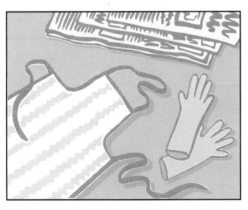

4. If you are printing or dyeing fabric, wear an overall or apron to stop your clothes from getting marked. It is also a good idea to wear rubber gloves so that your hands don't get stained with dye.

5. Remember to put the tops and lids back on paints and glues to stop them from drying up. Wash any glue off your fingers so that you don't leave mucky finger marks.

6. If you want the things you make to look really bright and shiny, sew or glue on sequins, felt shapes, ribbons, diamantés, beads and buttons. You can find them in most department stores.

PAINTED PILLOW CASES

Have you ever thought of designing your own pillowcase for your bed? All you need is a plain white or coloured pillowcase and some fabric felt tip pens. Cover it with stars or moons that will never wash out, like the one below, or design your own pattern. Try drawing a picture of yourself fast asleep on your duvet cover or sheet as well.

Look at your own pyjamas or nightdress to get an idea of how to paint a picture of yourself.

Things you need

A plain pillowcase, duvet cover or sheet
Thin cardboard and a pencil or chalk
A pair of scissors
Fabric felt tip pens (including a black one)
Newspaper
Masking tape
Small sponge or toothbrush

Try dabbing lots of different colours on to your pillowcase.

Seeing stars

1. Draw seven large star shapes and ten small ones on some thin cardboard. Carefully cut them out with a pair of small scissors. Slip newspaper inside the pillowcase to stop the paints running.

2. Arrange the card shapes on one side of the pillowcase. Then, with a small sponge or toothbrush, dab or splatter fabric paint around the shapes. Let the paint dry before you decorate the other side.

3. Use different colours on top of each other to get a really bright effect. Let the paints dry and then take out the newspaper. Turn the pillowcase inside out and iron it well to fix on the design.

HANDY HINTS

To stop the pillowcase moving while you are drawing on it, tape it across the corners to a table or the floor.

Your pictures will look much neater if you draw in one direction when you colour them with fabric felt pens.

Instead of using fabric felt tips, you can use fabric paint. The pens are easier to use, but the paint will go further. For big areas, dab on paint with a sponge.

Counting sheep pillowcase

A body in your bed

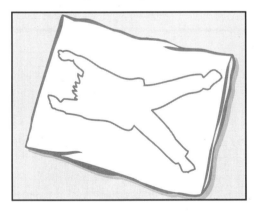

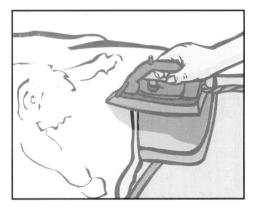

1. Lay a white duvet cover on the floor and put flat sheets of newspaper inside it. Lie on top of the duvet with your arms stretched out. Ask a friend to draw around you with a soft pencil or chalk.

2. Stand up carefully. Make sure the shape is exactly how you want it to be. Then carefully go over the outline with a black fabric felt tip pen. Add details, such as hair, a face, clothes or pyjamas.

3. Fill in the design with brightly-coloured fabric felt tip pens or fabric paints. Let them dry and then take out the newspaper. Turn the duvet cover inside out and iron it well to fix on the design.

POTATO PRINT PANTS

You have probably already printed with cut-out potato shapes and paint on paper. Why not use the same idea to brighten up your boxer shorts or pants. Instead of using poster paint, you will need special fabric paint and some big potatoes or carrots to cut up into different patterns.

Things you need

Boxer shorts or pants
Fabric paint and a paintbrush
A felt tip pen
A small vegetable knife
Masking tape and newspaper

Glue short pieces of spaghetti on to a piece of thick card. Brush paint over them and print lines over the potato prints.

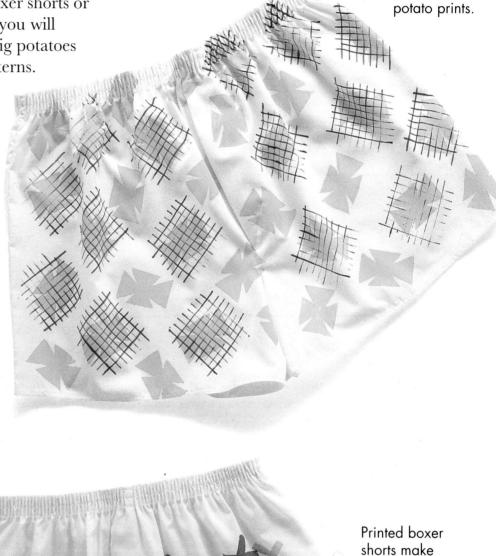

Use different-sized potatoes to make big and small shapes of the same design.

Printed boxer shorts make good presents.

8

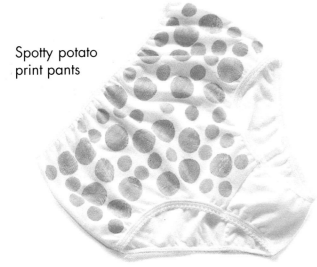

Spotty potato print pants

HANDY HINTS

When you are cutting shapes in a potato, make sure you cut away from your body. Shapes without curves, such as a star or cross, are the easiest to cut.

To get an even colour, spread the fabric paint on to the potato cut-out with a paintbrush. Do not brush on too much paint or the pattern will smudge.

Hearts and kisses

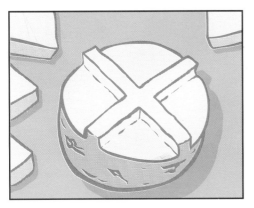

1. Carefully cut a big potato in half, widthways. Draw a big cross on one half with a felt tip pen. Then cut around the cross and cut away the rest of the potato so that the cross stands out, as shown.

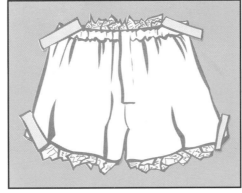

2. Stuff a pair of boxer shorts with newspaper to stop the paint from running. Then tape the shorts to a table top or the floor. Dab the cut potato with a tissue to mop up any extra potato juice.

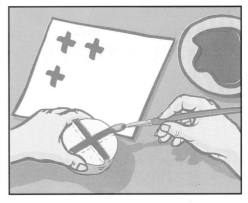

3. Brush paint on to the potato cut-out. Turn the potato over and print the pattern on to some paper to test it. If it looks good, print as many crosses as you want on to the boxer shorts.

4. Now cut a different pattern out of the other half of the big potato, such as a diamond or heart shape, like this. Brush a different colour paint on to the heart and print this pattern on to the shorts.

5. When the prints are dry, turn the shorts over and print on the back. Leave the shorts to dry. Then turn them inside out. Iron the shorts on the inside to fix the paint so that it won't wash off.

6. You can use carrots to print spots in lots of different colours. Cut off the top and brush paint on to the cut end. Use big carrots to print big spots and little, baby carrots for small spots.

COOL CAPS AND HATS

These two pages show you how to make plain hats, caps or berets look extra special and colourful. There are lots of ideas on how to decorate them with studs, puff paint and jazzy diamantés and sequins. You can also cover them with all sorts of bright felt shapes.

Things you need

A cap or felt beret
Diamantés, studs
 and puff paints
Brightly-
 coloured felt
Scissors and
 fabric glue
Ribbon
Tracing paper
A black felt tip pen
 and a pencil
Pins
Paper

Fruit salad beret

Flower power hat

Fruit salad beret

1. To make this fruit salad beret, first draw your design on some paper. Draw any fruit you like, such as strawberries, oranges, grapes and bananas.

2. Trace over the shapes of each fruit on to separate pieces of tracing paper. Pin the tracing paper shapes on to the right coloured felt and cut them out.

3. Arrange the felt fruit shapes on the top of the beret. Pin them in place. Glue the back of each shape and then stick them down in the right position.

Puff paint cap

Use a simple design, such as squiggles and dots, when you decorate a cap with puff paint. To make the paint puff up faster, heat it with a hair dryer.

Sparkling studs

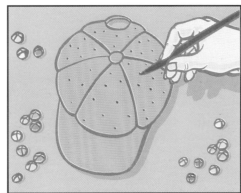

Before you start, mark where you want the studs to go on the hat with a felt tip pen. Push each stud from the front to the back of the cap, and then close them.

Flower power

To make a very pretty hat, cover a straw or felt hat with brightly-coloured felt flowers, bows or ribbon rose buds. Stick or sew them around the brim of the hat.

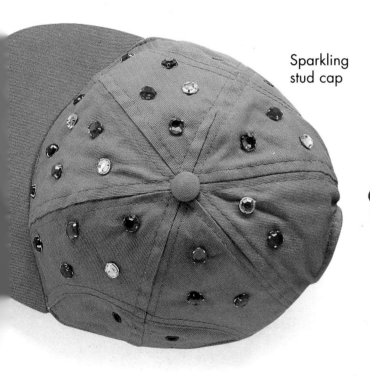

Sparkling stud cap

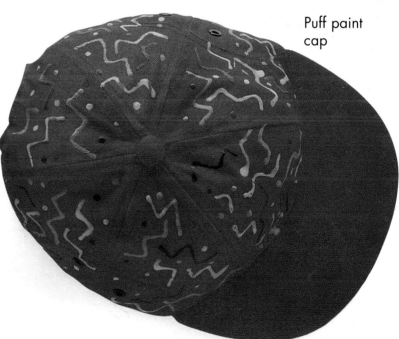

Puff paint cap

HANDY HINTS

The prongs on studs are sometimes quite difficult to close. Try pushing each prong down with the blades of a pair of closed scissors.

When you are decorating a hat with felt shapes, arrange them and pin them into position before you stick them down.

GLOW-IN-THE-DARK BANNERS

Make your own banners that glow-in-the-dark to hang up in your bedroom. All you need is some black fabric and some special fluorescent fabric paints. You can decorate the banners with spooky monsters and ghosts or design a super space scene. The paints will glow for up to twenty minutes in the dark. To make them glow again just turn on the light for a few seconds.

Things you need

Black paper and coloured chalks
Black fabric, 95 cm long
  and 40 cm wide
Fluorescent fabric paints in
  bright colours
Old newspaper
Masking tape and fabric glue
Ribbon or string
Two pieces of thin dowelling,
  each about 45 cm long

Night-time scenes make good designs for glow-in-the-dark banners.

Out-of-this-world banner

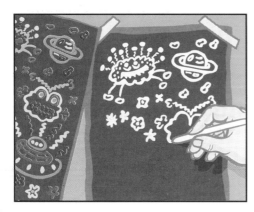

1. Before you begin, work out your design on black paper, using coloured chalks. Tape the black fabric to a table top. Then copy your design on to it with white chalk, as shown.

2. Go over the outline of your design with brightly-coloured fluorescent paints. Then fill in any details. Squeeze the tubes very gently so that the paint comes out slowly. Leave the paint to dry.

3. If you want to make your banner look extra shiny, add fake beady eyes, sequins or diamantés. To stick them on, put blobs of paint on the fabric and press the eyes into the paint.

HANDY HINTS

Glow-in-the-dark fabric paints usually come in plastic tubes with a nozzle. Do not press too hard as the paint will come out too fast and your designs may smudge.

It is a good idea to have kitchen paper or tissues handy to catch any drips while you are painting.

If you want to cover a large area with paint, spread it on with a piece of card or a flat ice cream stick.

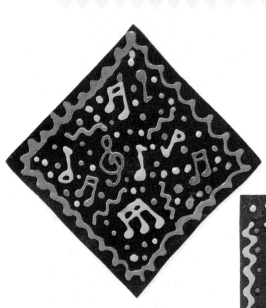

Make glow-in-the-dark badges to sew on your jacket or jeans.

Out-of-this world banner

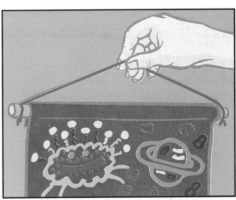

4. To make the banner, turn the sides of the fabric under by about 1 cm. Stick them down with fabric glue. Lay the fabric face down and put one piece of dowelling near the top edge, as shown.

5. Roll the fabric around the dowelling and glue it down firmly with fabric glue, as shown. Glue the second piece of dowelling to the bottom edge of the banner in the same way.

6. When the glue is dry, cut a piece of ribbon a little longer than the width of your banner. Tie the ends to the top dowelling, as shown. Hang the banner up in your bedroom and watch it glow.

A REALLY RAG DOLL

Here is a rag doll with a real difference. You can make it without any sewing at all. All you need are lots of colourful strips of fabric, string or wool, and a ball for the doll's head. It makes a very good present to hang on the wall or just to decorate someone's bed.

Really rag girl doll

Things you need

Pink, red and patterned fabric
Wool, string or thin ribbon
A small, soft ball
A pair of scissors

Strips of fabric	
Head/Body	7 pink strips 3 cm x 68 cm
Arms	16 strips 3 cm x 21 cm
Skirt	19 strips 3 cm x 60 cm
Bodice	1 long red strip 4 cm x 109 cm
Scarf	1 red square 22 cm x 22 cm

Rag girl

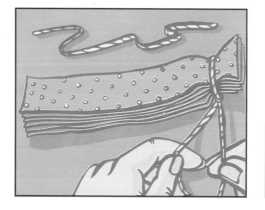

1. Cover the ball with the pink strips of fabric, three across and four in the other direction. Twist the strips at the neck and tie them together with wool.

2. Make a long bundle out of all the arm strips, as shown. Tie a piece of wool, about 3 cm from each end, to hold the strips of fabric together.

3. Divide the pink neck strips in half. Put the arms between them. Tie wool around the pink strips, like this, to hold in the arms at the waist.

14

Make a baby rag doll out of pink and white strips.

Use blue fabric to make this really rag boy doll.

Rag boy

4. Tie another piece of string loosely around the waist. Loop the skirt strips over it, one at a time. When they are evenly around the doll, tighten the string.

5. For a scarf, fold the square in half and tie it around the doll's head. Wrap the bodice strip around the neck, cross it over at the front and tie it at the back.

For a boy doll, divide the skirt strips in half. Leave one in the middle. Tie each half with wool. Tuck the middle strip between the legs and loop it over the waist tie.

15

FLYING ANGELS

On these two pages you can find out how to make cheerful flying angels out of scraps of cloth. They make wonderful decorations to hang on the Christmas tree, or just to hang on a wall. Instead of making an angel, you can leave the wings off to make a little cloth doll.

Things you need

About 0.5 m of white fabric
Yellow or patterned fabric
    for the dress
Paper, pencil and scissors
Pins, needle and thread
Red and black felt
    tip pens
Kapok (or wadding)
    for filling
Yellow embroidery
    thread
A small piece of
    thin ribbon
Scissors

Smiling
angel

Make a
big angel
for the
top of the
Christmas
tree.

Make different
coloured
angels.

Without the
wings the angels
turn into little
cloth dolls.

Smiling angel

1. Draw a simple doll shape, about 14 cm high, on a piece of paper. Then draw a wing shape, 19 cm long. Draw a 1 cm seam allowance all around the shapes. It will be a bit less between the legs.

2. Cut out the doll and wing shapes. Fold the white fabric in half and pin the shapes to it. Cut them out so you have two fabric doll shapes and two wing shapes. Take out the pins.

3. With the right sides facing, pin the doll shapes together and the wings together. Sew around the edges. Leave a gap down the side of the body and the wings. Turn them the right way out.

4. Fill both the body and the wings with wadding or kapok and sew up the gaps. Draw a big T - shape, like this, on some paper to fit over the angel's body. This is her dress pattern. Cut it out.

5. Fold the yellow fabric in half and pin the dress pattern on to it. Cut out two dress shapes. With the right sides facing, sew along the shoulders and down the sides. Turn the dress the right side out.

6. Slip the dress on the angel. Gather in the neck and neaten all the edges. Then sew on the wings and a ribbon loop. Draw on a face. Make her hair by sewing on tiny knots of embroidery thread.

HANDY HINTS

When you are making the angel's body pattern, draw the head straight on to the body without giving her a neck. This makes it easier to turn the angel the right way around.

To make an angel that really glitters, sew or glue sequins and diamantés on to her clothes.

If you don't have any kapok for wadding, you can use cotton wool instead. Use the blunt end of a pencil to push it into the arms and legs.

Instead of making the hair out of embroidery thread, you can make long hair out of strands of wool and short hair out of furry material.

CRAZY TIE-DYE

Now you can make your own special tie-dye T-shirts covered with all sorts of crazy and exciting designs. All you need is some strong string and some brightly-coloured fabric dyes. The great thing about tie-dye is that no two designs are ever the same.

Things you need

A light coloured T-shirt
A bucket and water
Cold water fabric
  dye and dye fix
A wooden spoon
Salt
Thin string
Vinegar
Apron
  and
  rubber
  gloves

Crazy tie-dye T-shirts

Tie-dye T-shirt

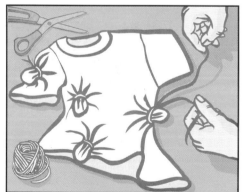

1. First wash the T-shirt you are going to tie-dye. Then gather a little clump of the shirt and tie it with strong string. Make a very tight knot. Make little clumps all over the shirt, as shown.

2. Dissolve the dye in a jug of warm water and stir it for a few minutes. Fill the bucket with cold water. Then, in a jug, mix four tablespoons of salt with the packet of special dye fix.

3. Pour the dye mixture and the dye fix and salt mixture into the bucket. Stir them together well. Drop the T-shirt into the bucket of dye and push it down. Keep stirring it for about ten minutes.

Tie-dye a long piece of fabric to make a swirly scarf.

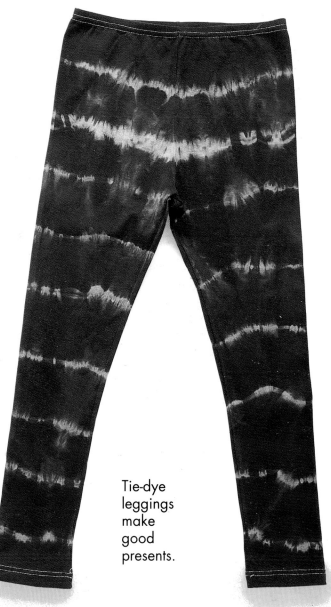

Tie-dye leggings make good presents.

4. Make sure that the T-shirt is completely covered with dye and leave it for fifty minutes. Stir from time to time. Then take it out and rinse it under cold water until the water runs clear.

5. Hang the T-shirt up to dry. When it is dry, undo the bundles of fabric. Now you can see the strange patterns all over the T-shirt. The best results seem to come from small, tight clumps.

6. Iron the shirt well to take out the wrinkles the knots have made. If you want a second colour, tie up a few new clumps. Repeat steps one to five with a darker colour fabric dye.

FROM OLD TO NEW

Have your favourite jeans got holes in them? Instead of mending them with plain patches, you can design your own fabric pictures to patch them with. All you need are scraps of brightly-coloured fabric and some colourful embroidery thread.

Things you need

A pair of blue jeans, a skirt
  or shorts
Scraps of fabric
Sewing thread, a needle
  and pins
Embroidery silks
Scissors

Make a patch pocket and sew it on to your skirt.

Embroider your initials on to your blue jeans.

Blanket stitch

1. Work from left to right with the thread at the top edge of the fabric. Point the needle upwards and push it through the fabric from front to back, like this.

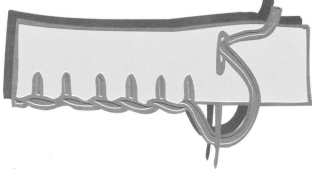

2. Pull the thread out between the fabric and the thread, as shown. Do this again and again until you have sewn along all the edges of the fabric shape. Try not to pull the thread too tight.

Before you sew on your patches, draw your design on some paper.

Pretty patches

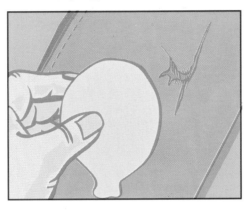

1. Measure the hole that needs patching. Then cut out a shape, such as this big, round balloon. Make sure it is a little bigger than the hole so that there is enough fabric to turn in.

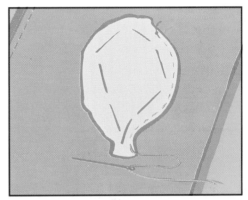

2. Carefully pin the shape over the hole and sew it down with large tacking stitches. Take out the pins. Then turn in the edges of the patch and sew them down with small running stitches, as shown.

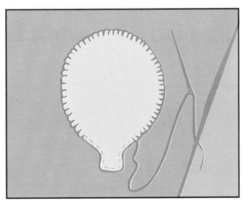

3. Decorate and neaten the edges with blanket stitch as shown in the box on the facing page. It is best to use two threads of embroidery silk at a time. Use a nice bright colour so that it shows up.

4. Add more shapes, such as a person or an animal. Cut out clothes shapes and sew them in a row to make a washing line. Embroider the line and add pegs to hold on the clothes.

SIMPLE SHOULDER BAGS

Instead of buying an expensive bag, why not make one for yourself. You can easily turn an old pair of blue jeans into a stunning shoulder bag decorated with felt, sequins, beads or paints. Make a neck purse out of scraps of fabric to carry money and other important things.

Things you need for a blue jeans bag

A pair of old blue jeans
Scissors and a tape measure
Pins and a needle
Button thread
A ballpoint pen

for a neck purse

A piece of fabric, 13 cm long
  and 20 cm wide
Narrow ribbon, 75 cm long
Embroidery thread, ribbon or lace
A needle and thread
Scissors and fabric glue
Fabric paints, buttons, sequins
  and felt for decoration

Cut out flower shapes from brightly-coloured felt and sew or glue them all over the front of your bag.

Blue jeans bag

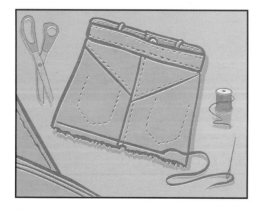

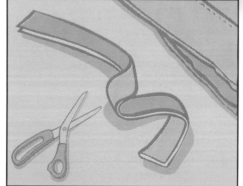

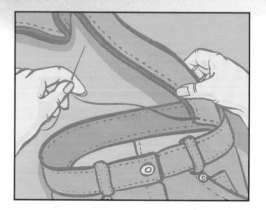

1. Turn the blue jeans inside out. Draw a line across them, where the legs meet the body. Cut along the line. Using a running stitch, sew along the bottom, like this, to make a bag.

2. To make a shoulder strap for the bag, cut a strip of material, about 60 cm x 10 cm, from one of the legs you have cut off. Then fold the strip of fabric in half along its length.

3. Turn both the edges of the strap in by 1 cm and pin them together. Sew along the edge. Then sew the two ends of the strap on to the inside of the blue jeans bag at the waist.

HANDY HINTS

Although you can glue some of the decorations on to your bag, it is best to sew the seams as they need to be strong.

If you are going to use fabric paints, draw the design on to the material with a soft pencil before you start painting.

You can also make a bag out of an old pair of shorts. Sew on a dressing gown cord for the shoulder strap.

Nifty neck purses

Nifty neck purse

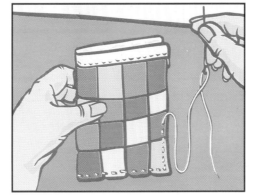

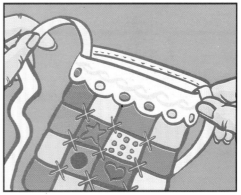

1. With the wrong side of the fabric facing you, sew the top edge down about 5 mm. Turn the fabric over and sew on a thin strip of lace. Decorate the fabric with buttons, puff paint and felt.

2. Fold the fabric in half, with the decorated sides together. Then sew along the bottom and the open side, about 5 mm from the edges, so that you have a small purse, like this.

3. Stitch one end of the narrow ribbon to one side of the purse, close to the top. Stitch the other end to the other side of the purse. Then turn the purse the right side out.

EASY WEAVING

These marvellous mats are woven out of small balls of brightly-coloured wool. They can be plain, stripy or patterned and are fun and easy to make with a home-made cardboard loom. You can also weave small coasters for glasses and cups, a bookmark and even a colourful purse.

Things you need

A piece of card (for the loom)
A ruler and pencil
A pair of scissors
A darning needle
Small balls of brightly
  coloured wool

Make a set of colourful stripy mats. Add pretty wool fringes.

A cardboard loom

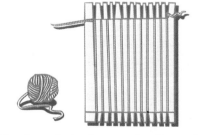

1. To make a loom, measure and cut a piece of stiff card (a cereal packet is ideal) slightly larger than you want your mat to be. This loom is 17 cm long and 13 cm wide.

2. Draw two long lines across the card, 2 cm from the top and 2 cm from the bottom. Mark short lines, 1 cm apart, as shown. Snip along the short lines to the long lines with small scissors.

3. To thread the loom, tie the end of some wool to the top left-hand corner. Wind on the warp so that it goes up and down the front of the loom and under the slits, as shown.

How to weave

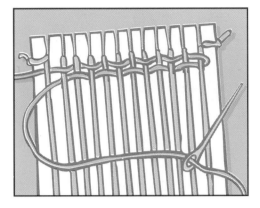

1. Thread the darning needle with wool and start weaving under and over the threads of the warp. For the next row, weave over the threads you went under and under the ones you went over.

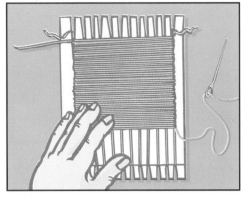

2. Repeat these two rows until you have woven the length of the loom. As you weave, gently push each row up close to the one above it to make sure the mat is nice and tight.

3. When you have reached the bottom of the loom, cut off the remaining wool and knot or glue down the end. Then carefully lift the mat off the loom so that you can use it again.

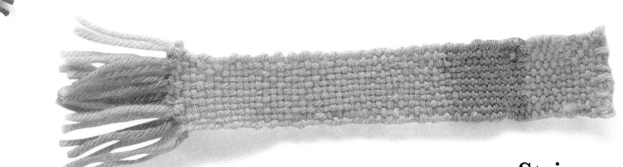

Weave some wool into a big bright bookmark.

Stripy mats

To make a purse, wind the warp thread on to the back and front of the loom. Weave on both sides of the loom with the weft wool doubled.

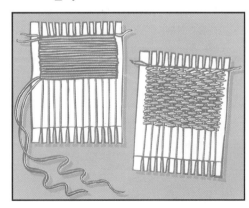

For horizontal stripes, weave five rows in one colour and two in another. Weave the colour you are not using into the side of the row you are working. To make vertical stripes, weave one row one colour and the next in another colour.

SMELLY SWEET BAGS

These smelly lavender bags look like big sweets. You can make them in different shapes and sizes out of scraps of plain or patterned fabric. Fill a basket full of smelly sweet bags as a pretty table decoration or a present, or put them into drawers to make your clothes smell nice and fresh. If you can't find any lavender, try using dried rose petals or pot pourri instead.

Things you need

Scraps of fabric, either plain or with
  small colourful patterns and prints
Dried lavender, rose petals or
  pot pourri
Thin coloured ribbon
  and thread
Scissors and pins
Fabric glue, such as Copydex
Lace or embroidery anglaise

Hang up a row of sweets glued or sewn on to some ribbon.

Make big sweets to scent your clothes.

Fill a basket with smelly sweet bags made from scraps of felt.

To make glittery sweets, use shiny fabric decorated with sequins, diamantés or glitter paint.

26

Sew a loop of cord on a sweet bag and hang it over a coat hanger.

HANDY HINTS

It is much easier to make the smelly sweet bags if you do not fill them too full of lavender or pot pourri.

Instead of using thread to tie up the ends of the sweets, you can use different coloured rubber bands or wool.

Smelly sweets

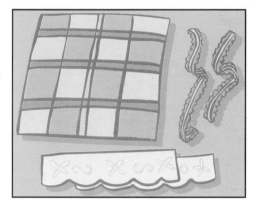

1. Cut out a piece of patterned fabric, about 10 cm wide and 10 cm long. Cut two pieces of narrow ribbon and two strips of lace or embroidery anglaise, each about 10 cm long.

2. Spread glue along the wrong side of one of the ribbons and one of the strips of lace. Stick them on to the right side of the fabric, along one edge, as shown. Do the same on the other edge.

3. When the glue is dry, stick a strip of fabric, about 3.5 cm wide and 10 cm long, on to the middle of the square piece of fabric, like this. Instead of fabric you could use a piece of wide ribbon.

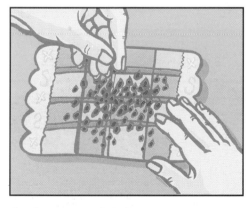

4. Turn the fabric square over and put a small pile of lavender or pot pourri in the middle. Then fold in the top and bottom edges so that you have a little sausage shape.

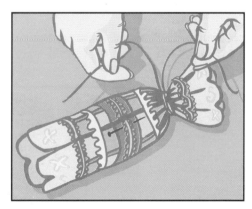

5. Hold the sausage shape together with a pin. Then break off a piece of strong thread and tie it tightly, about 2 cm from one end, as shown, so that it looks like a big sweet.

6. Put more lavender in the open end of the sweet if it is not full enough. Tie up the end. Take out the pin and trim off the thread. Then tie a bow of thin ribbon over the thread at each end.

PECULIAR POT HOLDERS

Oven mitts and gloves make good presents, especially when they look bright and cheerful, like this funny face mitt and slithery snake glove. If you line them with thick wadding, you can use them to hold hot pots, plates and dishes. But be careful not to put them close to a flame or they will burn.

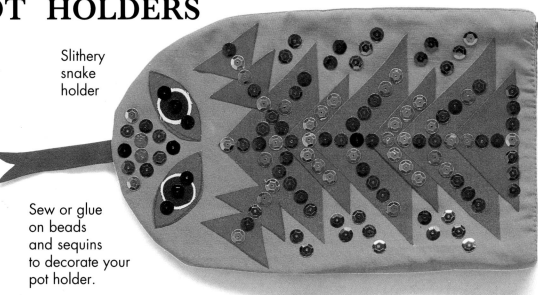

Slithery snake holder

Sew or glue on beads and sequins to decorate your pot holder.

Things you need

A pencil and paper
1 m of plain fabric
0.5 m of thick wadding
Scraps of brightly-coloured
  felt, beads and buttons
A needle and thread
Scissors and pins
Fabric glue
Thin ribbon

HANDY HINTS

It is easier to make pot holders without a thumb, but it is easier to hold on to hot things if they have one.

Make the gap in between the hand and the thumb extra big. Use a pencil to push the thumb the right side out.

To make a pot holder pattern which is big enough for an adult to wear, draw around an adult's hand.

Funny face

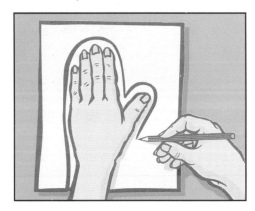

1. Draw around your hand on to a sheet of paper, keeping your fingers together, like this. Make the thumb extra big. Cut out the pattern, making it a little bigger all the way around.

2. Pin the paper glove pattern on to the plain fabric. Cut out four gloves, as shown. Then pin the pattern on to the thick wadding and cut out two more gloves exactly the same size, like this.

3. Pin two fabric gloves together with the right sides facing each other. Sew around three sides of the glove, as shown, 0.5 cm from the edge. Then turn the glove the right way around.

Funny
face pot
holder

Try making a
patchwork pot
holder out of lots
of scraps of fabric.

4. Sew a wadding glove on to each of the two remaining fabric gloves, as shown. Then, with the fabric gloves facing each other, make another glove as you did the first one.

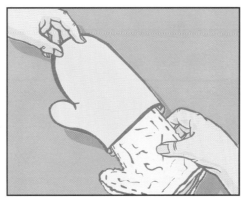

5. Keeping the glove inside out, slip it inside the first glove to make a thick lining. Fold in the edges of the inner and outer gloves at the wrist and sew them neatly together.

6. To make a funny face, cut out a felt mouth, eye and ear and some felt hair. Glue them on to the glove. Sew a loop of ribbon with a felt flower on to the bottom so you can hang up the pot holder.

FUNNY FINGER GLOVES

Turn a pair of woollen gloves into a pirate, a scarecrow, a soldier, a crazy clown and a happy man. Or design your own puppet gloves with animal or spooky fingertips. Make them for yourself or as a present for a friend. Small children will love wearing them.

Things you need

A pair of plain-coloured knitted gloves
Scraps of felt or fabric in bright colours
Wool, beads, buttons and ribbon
Scissors, a needle and thread
Fabric glue and tissue paper

Amazing animal glove

Funny finger people glove

Finger people

1. For a pirate little finger, cut out a round, pink felt head and a red nose. Cut out a brown beard, black eye and a black eye-patch. Stick the features on to the face and stick it on the glove.

2. Cut out two black felt hats. Stick one to the front of the finger and the other to the back so they cover the top of the head. Decorate the hat and tie a fabric scarf around the neck.

3. Make a scarecrow for the next finger. Cut out black felt eyes and a nose, a pink mouth and two brown hats. Stick yellow wool hair on to the head before you stick on the hats. Tie on a scarf.

4. The soldier on the middle finger has a pink face, black moustache, red nose and a black hat with a gold chin strap. Sew on four tiny gold beads to finish off his outfit.

5. Make the clown on the fourth finger with cross-shaped black eyes, a pink nose, a red mouth and a bright peak hat with a flower. Gather ribbon for his collar and sew buttons below it.

6. The smiling man on the thumb has a white shirt and collar, a red bow-tie and a blue felt jacket. Give him a pink face, little black eyes, a smiling mouth and fuzzy wool hair.

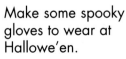

Make some spooky gloves to wear at Hallowe'en.

HANDY HINTS

To stop the glue sticking the fingers of the glove together, stuff each one with tissue paper before you start.

Make sure you do not sew the fingers together when you sew on the buttons or any other decorations.

Stick the nose, eyes and mouth on to the face before you stick the face on to the finger of the glove.

SUPER SOCKS AND SNEAKERS

With special fabric paints and felt tip pens you can make your sneakers look bright and cheerful, even if they are quite old. If you want them to look extra smart, you can decorate them with strips of shiny sequins. Try painting pictures and patterns on your socks as well, or decorate them with buttons, beads and tiny bells.

Things you need

Plain coloured sneakers
Plain coloured socks
Fabric paints and pens
Glitter and puff
  paints (if you like)
Fabric felt tip pens
Thin ribbon and
  ribbon bows
Buttons, beads and bells
Paper and a pencil
Newspaper and scissors

For really jazzy sneakers, glue on strips of sequins. Use bright metallic ribbon for the shoelaces.

Paint swirls of shiny puff paint on to canvas shoes.

Snazzy sneakers

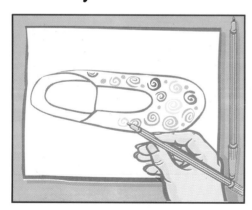

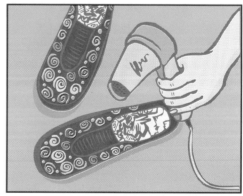

1. Before you start, decide what pattern you are going to paint on your sneakers. It is easier to paint a simple pattern, such as dots, stripes or squiggles. Draw your design on a sheet of paper.

2. Stuff the sneakers with old newspaper and start painting on the design. Paint one shoe before you start the other, working from the front to the back, like this. Use lots of different colours.

3. Squeeze little dots of puff paint in between the shiny swirls. Then let the paint dry. Use a hair dryer if you want the paint to dry faster. Then take the newspaper out of the canvas shoes.

Party
socks

Painted
socks

Jingling
socks

Super socks

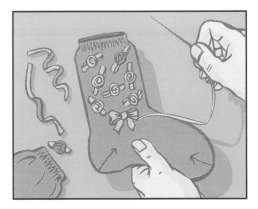

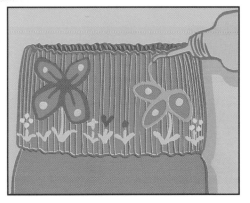

1. For pretty party socks, sew tiny ribbon roses around the top of plain socks. You can also make tiny bows out of thin, coloured ribbon and sew them on to the top of the socks, as shown.

2. Sew brightly-coloured beads around the top of a sock. These should only go as far as the ankle so they do not touch your shoes. If you would like noisy socks, sew on some tiny bells.

3. You can paint patterns on socks, using fabric paints, puff paints and felt tip pens. These do not wash off. If you want to make them really sparkle, use special fabric glitter paint as well.

PRETTY POM-POMS

These pretty pom-poms are simple and fun to make and can be any size you like. You can make them from all kinds of wool and use them to decorate hats, belts, hairbands and gloves. You can also make funny pom-pom people, fluffy animals and creepy crawly caterpillars or snakes.

Things you need

Thin card
A pencil and scissors
A cup or small plate
Small balls of brightly-
　coloured wool

Cover a hairband with sparkly pom-poms.

HANDY HINTS

It is best to use thin wool for small pom-poms and thicker wool for bigger, fluffy ones. The tighter you wind the wool around the cardboard circle, the fluffier your pom-pom will be. Try experimenting with different kinds of wool, such as mohair, wool with sparkles or even special speckled wool.

Sew different kinds of pom-poms together to make a creepy caterpillar.

Pretty pom-pom

1. Draw two circles on some thin card by drawing around a cup or small plate with a pencil. Draw a smaller circle in the middle of each big circle, like this.

2. Using small scissors, carefully cut out the two big circles of card. Then cut out the two small circles in the middle. Put one card ring on top of the other.

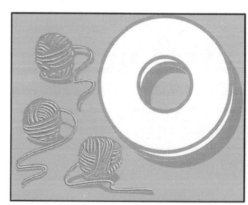

3. Wind a long piece of wool into a ball, small enough to go through the hole in the middle of the rings. Make two or three small balls of wool, like this.

Make extra big pom-poms for a woolly hat.

Brighten up your gloves with pretty pom-poms.

Make a chirpy yellow pom-pom chick.

Mixed-up pom-poms

Stripy pom-pom
To make stripy pom-poms, wind thin layers of different-coloured wool around the card rings, one on top of the other. Use four colours.

Dotty pom-pom
For dotty pom-poms, wind one layer of your main colour around the card rings. Add thin strips, like this, of another colour on every other layer of wool.

Squared-up pom-pom
For squared pom-poms, divide the rings into four quarters with a pencil. Cover each one with a different coloured wool.

Sparkly pom-pom
To make a pom-pom that sparkles, you need to buy special wool that looks as if it is full of tiny pieces of glitter.

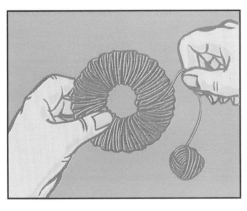

4. Wind the wool around the two card rings, as shown. Keep on winding until the rings are completely covered and only a tiny hole is left in the middle.

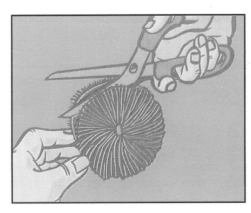

5. Then push one blade of the scissors between the two card rings, like this. Cut through all the wool around the edges. But be careful not to cut the card.

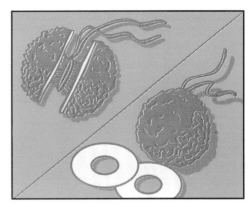

6. Pull the card rings slightly apart and wind a long piece of wool tightly around the middle of the pom-pom. Tie a tight knot. Then carefully pull off the card rings.

TERRIFIC T-SHIRTS

With a little imagination you can transform a plain white T-shirt into something much more colourful and fun to wear. Draw on your own design and decorate it with bright fabric paints, special puff paints, sparkling glitter paints or fabric felt tip pens.

Things you need

A white or plain
  coloured T-shirt
Paper and a
  pencil
Old newspapers
  and masking tape
Fabric paints, puff
  paints, glitter paints
  or fabric felt tip pens
Tailor's chalk or a very
  soft pencil
Embroidery transfers
  and carbon paper
An iron

Cover a T-shirt with different kinds of footsteps, using cut-out stencils.

Embroidery transfer T-shirt

Carbon copy T-shirt

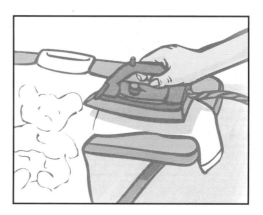

1. Before you start, draw your design on a big sheet of paper. Put a piece of carbon paper, ink side down, on to the front of a T-shirt. Put your design on top and trace over the design.

2. Take off the carbon paper. The design will show up on the shirt. Put sheets of newspaper inside the shirt and colour in your design with glitter paint, puff paints or fabric felt tip pens.

3. When the paint has dried, take out the newspaper and turn the T-shirt inside out. Iron over the design on the wrong side to fix the paint. Then it can be washed without coming off.

As a birthday present, give a friend a T-shirt with his age on the front.

Carbon copy t-shirt

HANDY HINTS

To stop the T-shirt moving while you are drawing on your design, tape it to a table top before you start.

Embroidery transfers usually come in a big sheet with lots of designs, letters and numbers. It is best to work out your design before you buy them.

Transfer T-shirt

1. Choose and buy the embroidery transfers you want to use for your design. Cut them out. Then tape them, one at a time, on to the front of the T-shirt, as shown. Make sure you put them ink side down.

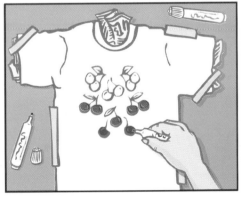

2. Carefully iron over the transfers using a hot iron. Then remove the paper. The designs will now be on your T-shirt. Colour them in with fabric paint, puff paint, glitter paints or fabric felt tip pens.

Permanent pictures

Make a picture on your T-shirt using different techniques, such as drawing, transfers and stencils. Use different pens and paints. Leave them to dry before fixing them with a hot iron.

QUICK-STICK PENCIL CASE

Make your own pencil case or wash bag quickly and easily without any sewing at all. All you need is some brightly-coloured PVC fabric, sticky-backed fabric and some velcro to keep it closed. You can also design a bigger bag for your swim suit and towel.

Things you need

Coloured or patterned fablon or
 any other sticky-backed fabric
Sticky-backed velcro, 22 cm long
Fabric glue
A ruler, ballpoint
 pen or pencil

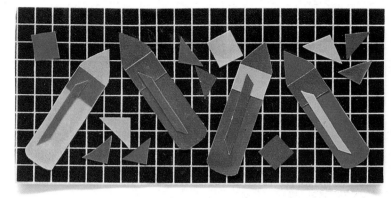

Quick stick
pencil case

Make your pencil case longer
if you want to fit in a ruler.

Perfect pencil case

1. Draw two rectangles, each about 22 cm long and 10 cm wide, on to the wrong side of the PVC fabric. Then draw a 1 cm margin around both rectangles, as shown. Cut out the bigger rectangles.

2. Peel the backing paper off a strip of velcro, 20 cm long. Stick it on to one of the long sides of one of the PVC rectangles. Stick velcro on to one of the long sides of the second rectangle.

3. To decorate the pencil case, cut out different shapes, such as these crayons, from fablon or sticky-backed fabric. Stick them on to the back and the front of the right side of the rectangles.

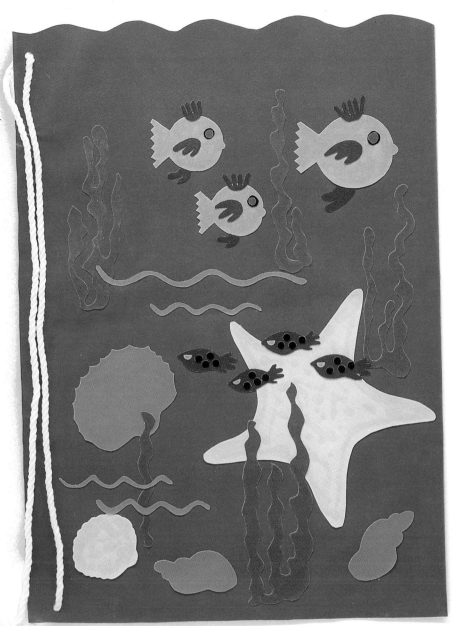

Decorate a swimming bag with fish and other sea creatures.

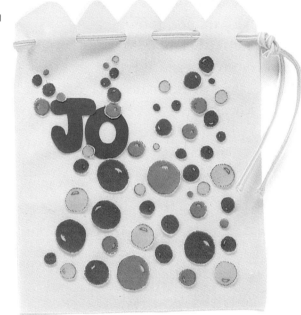

Stick your name on to your wash bag.

Laced-up case

Wash bag

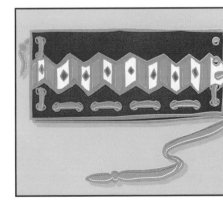

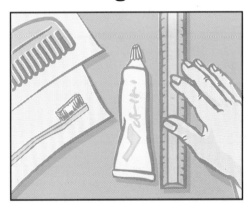

4. Spread glue around the three edges of one of the rectangles, on the wrong side, as shown. Line up the velcro so they match perfectly. Then stick the two rectangles together to make a pencil case.

As well as gluing the pencil case, you can tie it together with a shoe lace to make it even stronger. Use a hole punch around three of the edges and thread the shoelace through the holes, like this.

Make a wash bag in the same way as your pencil case. To work out the size, measure the things you are going to put inside, such as a toothbrush, comb, toothpaste and shampoo.

JOLLY JUGGLERS

All you need to make these jolly juggling balls are small pieces of felt and some dried peas, lentils or rice. Try making a tossed salad juggling set with a tomato, cucumber and green lettuce. Or give your friends a set of bright dice jolly jugglers.

Things you need

A pencil, paper and a ruler
Scissors and pins
Felt in bright colours
A needle and thread
Dried peas, beans, rice or lentil
Embroidery thread (for decoration)
Pinking shears

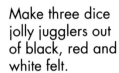

Make three dice jolly jugglers out of black, red and white felt.

Specially named jolly jugglers.

Tossed salad set

HANDY HINTS

Make a small paper funnel to use when you are filling your juggling balls. Do not overfill them or they may burst open at the seams.

If you do not have any felt, use any scraps of fabric you can find. Sew the fabric on the wrong side, to stop it from fraying. Then turn it the right way out.

Jolly
jugglers

Jolly jugglers

1. Draw six squares, each 5 cm long and 5 cm wide, on some paper. Cut out the squares and pin each one on to a separate piece of felt. Cut out the felt squares and take out the pins.

2. Sew three different coloured squares of felt together, as close to the edges as possible. Now you have a row of squares, like this. Do the same with the other three felt squares.

3. Sew the two rows of felt squares together so they form a cube shape, as shown. Leave one side open and fill the cube with dried peas or lentils. Then very neatly sew up the last side.

Tossed salad balls

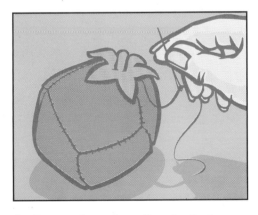

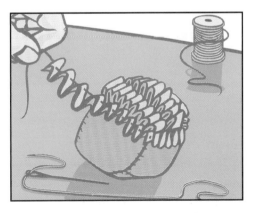

1. To make a juggling ball that looks like a tomato, make a cube shape using six squares of red felt. Cut out a small green star shape and sew it on to the top of the tomato as a stem, like this.

2. For a cucumber, cut two green crescent shapes and two petal shapes, about 16 cm long and 4 cm at the widest point. Sew them together, alternating the petal and crescent shapes.

3. Make a lettuce out of six 8 cm green felt squares sewn together into a cube. Cut out some extra strips of green felt with pinking shears. Gather the strips and sew them on to the lettuce cube.

AMAZING APRONS

Aprons make good presents as well as being very useful. On these two pages you can find out how to make your own and how to decorate it with pictures and patterns. There's a special cook's apron with lots of cooking tools, an artist's apron and a flowery apron for a gardener.

Things you need

0.5 m thick cotton fabric
4 x 50 cm cotton tape
  or strong, wide ribbon
A needle, pins and thread
A soft pencil and
  masking tape
Fabric pens and paint
A sheet of newspaper

Look in the kitchen to get an idea of the tools to paint on your crafty cook's apron.

Messy artist's apron

Crafty cook's apron

1. To make the paper pattern, draw a rectangle, 42 cm wide by 60 cm long, on some newspaper. Cut it out. Draw two lines, each about 10 cm long, 18 cm from the top of the rectangle.

2. Draw two lines from the two 10 cm lines, straight up to the top of the paper. On one side draw a big curve, as shown. Fold the paper in half lengthways and cut out the curve.

3. Open out the apron pattern. Pin it on the fabric and cut it out. For the pocket, cut a piece of fabric 28 cm wide and 18 cm deep. Turn under and pin the edges. Sew or glue them down.

HANDY HINTS

The measurements for the aprons are just a guide. You may want to make your apron bigger or smaller, longer or wider.

Hold a flat sheet of newspaper against you or the person you are making the apron for. Ask someone to help you measure the size you need.

Use fabric paints and puff paints to draw flowers on the busy gardener's apron.

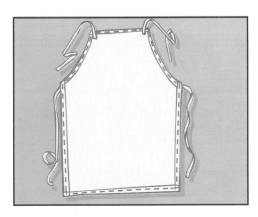

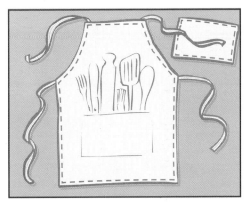

4. To neaten them, turn under and pin the edges of the apron. Sew or glue them down. Then sew the four cotton tapes in place, at the top and sides of the apron, as shown.

5. Pin the pocket in place and mark it with a pencil. Take it off. Tape the apron to a table and draw some cook's tools with a soft pencil. Make them look as if they are standing in the pocket.

6. Colour in the cook's tools with fabric pens and paint. Iron the back of the apron to fix the colours. Pin the pocket on to the apron and sew it in place, using a neat running stitch.

CRAZY CHRISTMAS STOCKINGS

On these two pages, you can find out how to make crazy Christmas stockings for all the family. It is best to use felt as it does not fray and is easy to decorate with sequins, beads and bits of fabric. As well as making big stockings, try making a string of little ones for each day of December to hang across the fireplace.

Things you need

Paper and a pencil
A pair of scissors
Large pieces of brightly-
    coloured felt
A large boot or sock
Pins, a needle and thread
Pinking shears
Beads, sequins, buttons,
    scraps of felt, ribbon
    and diamantés for
    decoration
Thin ribbon
Fabric glue

Super Santa
Stocking

Super Santa stocking

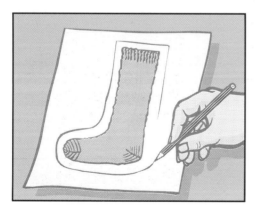

1. Lie a boot or big sock on a sheet of paper. Draw around it. Take the boot off the paper and cut out the boot pattern, making it a bit bigger all the way around.

2. Pin the paper pattern on to a big piece of red felt and then cut it out with pinking shears. Do this again so that you have two red felt boot shapes.

3. Draw a big Christmas tree shape on some paper. Cut it out and pin the pattern on to some green felt. Cut out the felt tree and take out the pins.

Stick different felt pictures on each of your tiny stockings.

Look in Christmas books to get an idea of how to decorate your stockings.

HANDY HINTS

Make sure all the decorations you have stuck on to the stocking are dry before you sew the front to the back. It is best to sew on things like buttons and bows.

You can make the stocking from other fabrics, but choose one that does not fray. Cut the edges with pinking shears.

4. Using paper patterns, cut a big pot shape out of felt for the tree to stand in. Then cut some parcel shapes out of different coloured felt, as shown.

5. Spread glue on the back of the tree shape and stick it on to one of the stockings. Stick the pot underneath the tree and the parcels around the pot.

6. Decorate the tree with sequins, diamantés and felt shapes. Sew the two sides of the stocking together with embroidery thread. Sew a loop of ribbon on the top.

45

COLOURFUL CHRISTMAS DECORATIONS

These Christmas decorations will make your tree look bright and cheerful and will last for a long time. You can make them in different shapes, such as stars, hearts and moons, from brightly-coloured felt, beads, sequins, buttons and ribbon. Hang them on your own tree or give them away as presents.

Things you need

Brightly-coloured felt
Wadding and thin ribbon
Diamantés, beads, glitter
  glue and sequins
Scissors or pinking
  shears
A needle, thread
  and pins
Paper, a pencil
  and fabric glue

Decorate the front and back of the decorations.

Use gold or silver thread to sew your decorations together.

Sparkling tree

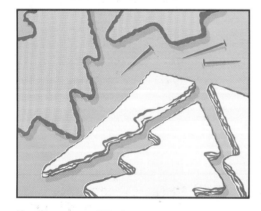

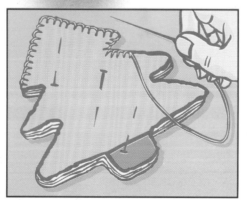

1. Draw a Christmas tree, about 12 cm tall, on some paper. Cut it out and pin it on a piece of green felt, folded in half. Cut out two felt trees. Then cut one tree shape from a piece of wadding.

2. Make a sandwich of the two felt trees with the wadding in the middle. Pin them all together and then sew them together, as close to the edges as possible, like this. Sew on a red felt pot.

3. Take out the pins and then decorate the tree as if it were a real tree. Sew or stick on beads, diamantés and strips of sequins. Sew a loop of ribbon on the top so you can hang up the tree.

Glitter stocking

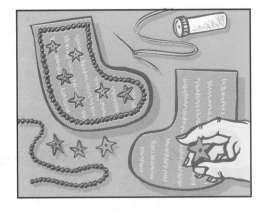

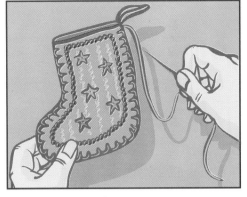

1. Using a paper pattern, cut two Christmas stocking shapes out of some red felt. Sew or glue a few sequins on to the shapes, leaving the edges free. Decorate the stockings with gold glitter glue.

2. Sew the two stocking shapes together, as close to the edge as possible. Leave the top open so that you can fill the stocking with tiny presents. Sew a loop of ribbon to the top of the stocking.

Hearts and stars

Make lots of heart, moon and star decorations, following the same directions as the sparkling Christmas tree. Decorate them with strips of sequins, glitter glue and diamantés.

Sequin stars, hearts and moons

HANDY HINTS

To give the decorations pretty edges, cut out the felt shapes with a pair of pinking shears.

These decorations are stuffed with wadding to make them look nice and thick. Or you can stick two pieces of felt together instead.

If you are not very good at sewing, cover the line of stitching with beads, braid or a strip of sequins.

You can buy sequins in many different shapes and sizes.